America's Culture War

2020 DiVision

Stephen Grant

AMERICA'S CULTURE WAR: 2020 DIVISION

Copyright © 2019 Stephen Grant

1405 SW 6th Avenue • Ocala, Florida 34471 • Phone 352-622-1825 • Fax 352-622-1875
Website: www.atlantic-pub.com • Email: sales@atlantic-pub.com
SAN Number: 268-1250

No part of this publication may be reproduced, stored in a retrieval system, or transmitted in any form or by any means, electronic, mechanical, photocopying, recording, scanning, or otherwise, except as permitted under Section 107 or 108 of the 1976 United States Copyright Act, without the prior written permission of the Publisher. Requests to the Publisher for permission should be sent to Atlantic Publishing Group, Inc., 1405 SW 6th Avenue, Ocala, Florida 34471.

Library of Congress Cataloging-in-Publication Number: 2019044672

LIMIT OF LIABILITY/DISCLAIMER OF WARRANTY: The publisher and the author make no representations or warranties with respect to the accuracy or completeness of the contents of this work and specifically disclaim all warranties, including without limitation warranties of fitness for a particular purpose. No warranty may be created or extended by sales or promotional materials. The advice and strategies contained herein may not be suitable for every situation. This work is sold with the understanding that the publisher is not engaged in rendering legal, accounting, or other professional services. If professional assistance is required, the services of a competent professional should be sought. Neither the publisher nor the author shall be liable for damages arising herefrom. The fact that an organization or Web site is referred to in this work as a citation and/or a potential source of further information does not mean that the author or the publisher endorses the information the organization or Web site may provide or recommendations it may make. Further, readers should be aware that Internet Web sites listed in this work may have changed or disappeared between when this work was written and when it is read.

TRADEMARK DISCLAIMER: All trademarks, trade names, or logos mentioned or used are the property of their respective owners and are used only to directly describe the products being provided. Every effort has been made to properly capitalize, punctuate, identify, and attribute trademarks and trade names to their respective owners, including the use of ® and ™ wherever possible and practical. Atlantic Publishing Group, Inc. is not a partner, affiliate, or licensee with the holders of said trademarks.

Printed in the United States

PROJECT MANAGER: Meaghan Summers
INTERIOR LAYOUT AND JACKET DESIGN: Nicole Sturk

50 percent of the royalties will be donated to Batson Children's Hospital in Jackson, MS.

Table of Contents

Preface 1

Chapter 1   To Serve or Be Served 5

Chapter 2   The Example of the Past 7

Chapter 3   Victim Culture creates Victims 11

Chapter 4   To Revert or To Be Redeemed 15

Chapter 5   Power and Responsibility 19

Chapter 6   Why Can't You Just Meet Me in the Middle? 23

Chapter 7   What is Love? 29

Chapter 8   We Are One 33

Chapter 9   Don't Be a Parrot 35

Chapter 10   Polarization 37

Chapter 11   Obstacles and Temptation 39

Chapter 12   Cell Phones-the Newest Temptation 41

Chapter 13	Sex Politicized	43
Chapter 14	A Fatherless Society?	47
Chapter 15	Morality of the Unborn	49
Chapter 16	Adoption as a Lifeline	53
Chapter 17	Fair and Impartial Criticism	55
Chapter 18	Hard work and Focus	59
Chapter 19	Immigration	61
Chapter 20	What is the Truth (and Can We Handle It)?	63
Chapter 21	The Hypnotized Never Lie	65
Chapter 22	A Higher Purpose	67
Chapter 23	To Search and to Strive	69
Chapter 24	Tax and Spend	71
Chapter 25	Trade Deficits and Policies	73
Chapter 26	Let's Compromise our Way to a More Perfect Union	75
Chapter 27	What About Congress?	77
Author Bio		81

Preface

My dear colleagues of the United States of America, I am a citizen just like you who desires peace. I have a family just like you do. We want to protect them and give them the best possible future. I'm certain you remember your youth. If you are as old as I am, you can remember roaming your neighborhood without care. You could depend upon those around you to watch over your kids, your house, and the things that mean the most to you. Neighbors meant something back then. We had neighborhood parties, and we shared meals together in the cul-de-sac.

Lately, I have seen people tear each other down. Slander pervades internet postings. Internet trolls post with no regard for the effect of their words. I have posted some awful comments, too. Those postings sow bitter discord and reap the same. Some of our children have become accomplices to the politics of hate while others have seen through the cruelty to bring new meaning to our society.

The idea of making friends out of our neighbors seems more alien than ever before. As a young boy, I knew the name of every family in my neighborhood. I could tell you the ages and even the middle names of all my friends. Now, I only know the names of my closest neighbors—for security and support only. We like to choose our friends based on our own likes and dislikes. Geography used to force us to hold our tongues when a difficult neighbor stopped by. Now, we avoid anyone we disagree with. I know that my children follow my actions. I want to teach them to listen to dissenting points of view and learn from them.

Our speed of life increases every year and, like good capitalists, we strive and we compete to have the smartest kids in the best school district with the most parks and recreation. We flee from neighborhoods in need and leave behind a simpler and less costly life for the more demanding fast lane. So, too, do our children find themselves deep in debt when they graduate. The cost of education is skyrocketing while the lessons learned are controlled more and more by only one side of the moral spectrum.

There is a problem. Our sons have acted out civil strife—heartbreaking and soul-tearing acts of violence at our schools and our busiest neighborhoods. Something has gone wrong with our American dream. Our children are learning something new that we did not intend to teach them. They have learned intolerance and hate. They have learned bigotry and hostility. They have learned that money and status are the goals of life. I see it when my friend and I hold doors open as a courtesy; those walking through chose not to enter through my black friend's door.

When we talk about each other, our words are sharp, and our concern for each other is dull. Most of the things I see are not new. They are amplified by the internet, though. You can post to everyone on Facebook for free, although that's a great way to make a fool of yourself to a lot of people. On one hand, cyberbullying pervades our society. On the other hand, the internet remains a wonderful tool for meeting people, discussing obscure topics, and sharing common interests.

As a Christian, I have been using the morals and values taught to me in school and church as a basis for my posts and blogs. An old acquaintance responded to one of my posts by suggesting I am contracting Alzheimer's! I happen to know that her political stance leans to the left and mine leans to the right. I also know that she is a strong and kind woman whom I respect. How, then, do I take her response? Simply calling someone names when fully grown is not helping the social fabric around us. Offering no proof or reasoning for a dissenting point of view is irresponsible, and it causes division. We are in a culture war, and we are the combatants.

These new challenges might seem enough for us to bear. Sadly, there is more. Our protests seem less about the greater good and more about winning at all costs. They seem more contrived and less about the facts. We have slipped from social and political correctness into social shaming and control politics. Our children see us shriek at the top of our lungs, and what does that teach them? They do as you *do,* not as you say. Every parent at least knows that.

Paid-for civil disobedience has taken over the airwaves—crowds and mobs funded by those with an agenda. Even the media outlets are spouting political jargon and partisan talking points. Since when did we allow our free press to become a bought-and-paid-for press?

My hope is that I can bring people together while discussing the ideas currently in play in the social fabric of our great country. I hope for the best in all people. I know I'm not perfect, but I search and strive for the best in myself. I wish to provide an independent and patriotic viewpoint from the middle class, which is grounded in faith and love. I hope to restore our desire for the greater good. I want to find the middle ground in our divided world. Let's be less concerned with power and more concerned with our youth.

In this brave new world, you can take the red pill, or you can take the blue pill. I'm suggesting you take neither pill and think for yourselves. Remember what made this country great: freedom of speech, freedom of religion, freedom of assembly, a strong work ethic, and deep abiding faith. I pray that my words will have value and will move our moral compass forward.

CHAPTER 1

To Serve or Be Served

There is only one you. You are beautiful, and there is no one else like you. I tell my kids that there is a difference between knowing that you are unique and deciding that you are special. Sometimes, we confuse the support of our family and friends. We take their love and generosity in the wrong manner. Do I think I am special and deserving? That depends on what I give the world in return. If I earn my way toward success, I can expect to feel deserving of it. Bob Dylan sang "Gotta Serve Somebody" and reminded everyone listening that, whether you're serving the Devil or God himself, serving is a necessity.

To serve somebody does not mean to be a slave. To serve somebody means to give them support, love, labor, and any talent and gifts you might have. The religious right wants us to serve one another with personal responsibility in mind. In earning another's trust through service, we gain our own freedom. Others see our inner strength and character and will give us the break we are looking for. The Progressive left has compassion for the public and seeks to improve the overall well being of our society. If we can assume that both sides have the good of the people in mind, we need not be concerned. We can find common ground in the betterment of society. So, why are we in the midst of a culture war? Let's review the biggest cause for relationship issues—money.

The religious right say that nothing comes for free. They should know, because the richest already pay the most in taxes. Our tax rate is progressively higher for each tax bracket upward in pay scale. Whether we live in a socialistic or a capitalistic society, the money comes from the people. Do you want a free college education … here you go! Do you want free medical care … here you go! The taxes and the deficit go up and up and up. It's the middle and upper classes that end up paying the bill. The Progressive left knows that the cost of national defense does not support their compassionate aims. To win elections, the left needs to support its base, which includes higher taxes for private citizens and corporations to fund social programs. The left despises reduced regulations, which can result in disaster if not handled properly. There is room for compromise here, but, in this current election season, there is much at stake. The future of our country is set by the presidency. The power of the executive branch has increased. We can't expect compromise now. It's a culture war, and the state of our economy, jobs, safety, and rights and your decisions make the difference.

Remember that there are always strings attached. There is no free lunch. Whether you lean left or right, you need to understand that politicians don't control the weather. They don't control the economy. They don't control your household or how you run it. They don't even control your vote, even though Hollywood and the media do their best to affect your thoughts. Our economy, jobs, and safety are strong. There is no need, at this time, for compassionate causes. The people are earning a good living, and the stock market is hot.

I do worry about those who cannot help themselves. When I give my labor to my community, I provide a service. We should volunteer for a greater cause than ourselves. Remember President Kennedy's Inaugural Address? He said, "Ask not what your country can do for you; ask what you can do for your country." That sentiment doesn't change with the seasons. It doesn't change with different administrations. Sacrifice for your neighbor is the highest form of love. Serving others is the main purpose of the government and our media, entertainers, engineers, and even managers and business owners. I wonder, sometimes, if that's what we are truly doing.

CHAPTER 2

The Example of the Past

I've seen deep hurt and felt deep cultural bonds when I moved to Mississippi. The people of Mississippi, no matter their skin color or heritage, have endured a terrible history. I've learned a few things about slavery and all of its wicked ways. Sad eyes and crooked crosses put fear into the working population of Blacks. Labor stolen from them by force. You can imagine the worst, and it probably happened here in Mississippi to the Black culture. What amazes me is the deep family ties among the beautiful Black families I have met here. Yes, they are dysfunctional, but whose family isn't? I was hesitant to move from Michigan to Mississippi. It was a job that brought me here, and a marriage and family have kept me here. While making the best of my new life, I have visited Baptist Churches, Catholic Churches, and Methodist Churches. I have worshiped with all creeds and colors. The music and the closeness I have felt here rivals, and sometimes surpasses, anything I have witnessed in the rest of the world. Mississippi is the home of the blues. It is also the home of gospel music.

The blues was born here for a reason. Deep pain, handed down for generations, can be felt. It's tangible in the eyes and the speech of those you meet here. The pain can be seen by visiting the Civil Rights Museum in Jackson. I lost my father when I was only 15 years old. That sorrow still does not compare to the life-altering pain felt by those in bondage. It affects you and makes you think. *How can I make sense of the senseless loss and suffering experienced in the past and the present?* We cannot always make sense of life. We may not always understand what our purpose in this world may be. Sometimes, we can look back on our life and, through reflection, understand that the sum of our total experiences makes us ready to be more useful to our community. I know that I never would have met my wife if not for losing that job in Michigan and moving to Mississippi.

From the pain and sorrow sprouted the most heartfelt and grace-filled music of our world (in my humble opinion). Gospel mixed with African tribal music spawned an escape of heartbreak through melody. Music lovers take pilgrimages to the Blues Trail in Mississippi, and they also find their way to the Civil Rights Museum. The story of grace in the midst of suffering is a powerful tale that needs to be told. The enduring love of the abolitionists changed the south. The day-to-day struggle of the people here, with the help of visionaries such as Dr. Martin Luther King Jr., Emmett Till, and Medgar Evers helped make the changes permanent. It's the people who endured the suffering and hardship that we must not forget. Their example should show us that, even in the midst of the darkest night, we can hope for a new dawn and a new day.

A new light is shining here, and, for the families of Mississippi, it is a beautiful light. Visitors come and learn of the deep roots and learn about the deep culture set forth in our country's heartland. From pain came grace and beauty. So is the tragic life that we live. We must struggle and strive for the best and the truth in each of our lives. In that struggle to improve ourselves, we gain purpose and achieve some sense of grace. If we reach out, we can lift up others around us. We can be a light to others who may unknowingly live in the darkness. Selflessness guided the civil rights leaders to lay down their lives for their fellow man. Great evil takes great sacrifice to overcome.

The reason Mississippians developed such beauty is that they had no other outlet. They could not walk away. Their lives were held captive, and making music was one of the few ways they could express their anxiety and hurt. We, in contrast, can run from the evil set upon us. We are not captives—we own our freedom. I was able to escape my lack of work in Michigan by moving out of state. Sometimes, you need to take a leap of faith before you find true love and happiness.

CHAPTER 2:

What, in response, are we doing in our daily lives as an example of love, grace, and community giving? What a challenge we have before us today. The experiment of the United States of America continues. How shall we carry forward the torch of freedom that our ancestors have handed to us?

You can plan, create, strategize, and carry out a grand scheme. You are not the sum of the things that happen to you. You can think for yourself. You can create tools and clothes and artwork, and you can fix things. You are a wondrous and beautiful being like none other on earth. You are a human being. You are powerful. I have seen people reform their lives in a matter of eight years or less. A friend of mine changed from drunk and divorced to sober and married within five years. As he was holding his newborn in his arms, watching the Fourth of July fireworks, I thought to myself, *they are more beautiful than the fireworks.*

I make these points, because Progressive Democrats in America want to perpetuate the belief that you are weak. They say, "Yes, you are a victim. There is no way out unless you get help from us, the government. You deserve the best, and we will give it to you." If you believe that, the hook is set, and those in power are reeling you in. Help can be found at the corner of your street. There's a church with good people who can help you get on your feet. There are short-term government programs that you can use to get out of poverty. Use them, but don't depend on them. If you become dependent, you have lost your freedom.

CHAPTER 3
Victim Culture Creates Victims

Today, 73.7 percent of U.S. citizens claim to be Christian. When I sit in my church and look around, I would expect it to be full, like on Christmas. To be a Christian, you need to study, understand, and practice the Word (the Bible). Why should you believe anything the Bible has to say? Here is why: the Bible is a collection of wisdom passed down by generations. There is truth, honor, loyalty, kindness, and, most of all, sacrifice in the stories. Whom, or what, do you follow? So many Christians don't practice their faith or attend church. Many don't really know what the Bible says about any certain topic. A Christian is supposed to invite their neighbors to church. A Christian is supposed to stand up for morals, virtues, and truth. Where, I ask you, are the Christians these days? Our country's morality is being attacked, and we are needed more now than ever before.

How is morality being attacked, you ask? Government-paid abortions, government-validated blurring of sexual identity, and government allowances for illegal immigration and sex trafficking invalidate the sanctity of life. I'll expand on these in later chapters. I wonder, *what are we replacing God with? Where are we sending our tithes? Who are we serving? Where else can we get lessons in morality than our local churches and church families?*

> *"By the sweat of your brow, you will eat your food until you return to the ground."*
>
> —Genesis 3:19

"The world belongs to the energetic."

—Emerson

"Without labor, nothing prospers."

—Sophocles

"Those who work their land will have abundant food, but those who chase fantasies will have their fill of poverty."

—Proverbs 28:19

Don't sit back and say, "I'm going to speak of my faith but do nothing." We should show our faith by serving and tending to others, for faith without works is dead. This is the compassion of the religious right. If we serve each other, we do not need high taxes, big government, or socialism. If we care for our neighbors and prevent harm from coming to them, we can avoid the deep pain that leads to immorality.

So many of us wander through life with no direction. No purpose. No guiding principles. Are you working paycheck to paycheck? Are you in debt up to your eyeballs? You are not the sum of your wins and losses. You can be more. When I first started working in the automotive industry, I witnessed negotiations by the labor union demanding higher salaries while selling out their future. I was awestruck by the greed of the moment. We can see, now, the result of their shortsightedness. Unions are losing ground in American industry. I used to think that collective bargaining was useful. The history of unions, unfortunately, has been marked by collecting dues with little service in return. I don't support unions due to their past offenses against companies, communities, and their members. That's an important lesson, but a very costly lesson our country has learned. Our House of Representatives has exemplified similar offenses by using any means possible to delegitimize a sitting president in order to win back the executive branch for the Democratic National Convention (DNC). Their recent offenses against the executive branch parallel the actions of the unions in the '80s and '90s. In this case, the Progressive Democrats are selling out to power and money for short-term gain. I know. You believe it is the other way around. You believe the president is the problem. Where, I ask you, is the proof? Where are the documents showing wrongdoing? When will you start listening to both sides of the argument and make a decision for yourself? I get it; you don't like the tweets and the ungentlemanly words President Trump uses. He is a New York City scrapper who has fought his way through life. I'm not a Trump apologist, but I understand that, when you are attacked constantly, you need to fight back. The media won't repeat Trump's words, so he must use Tweets.

We come from strong immigrants who moved from abusive governmental systems. Those immigrants entered our nation legally, and they forged a new nation. Your ancestors had a vision for a more perfect union, and they created it by the sweat of their brow and a hard-fought revolution. You now live in the most successful and most powerful country in the world. That makes you the inheritor of the most amazing gift in the history of this world. Will you honor their gifts by working hard, striving for your best, and creating? Or will you, as a victim would do, ask for a handout and live out of the government's hand? It is in your power to earn your own living. It is in your power to pay off your debts. According to Bureau of Economic Analysis, our current economy is growing by 3.1 percent in the second quarter and 2 percent in the third quarter. This is great news! Personal income has increased as well from 0.1 percent in July to 0.4 percent in August, 2019. It's time to rise, better yourself, and don't dishonor your ancestors or yourself. Galatians 6 says, "A man reaps what he sows."

How does victimhood serve the greater good? I don't enjoy watching talking heads on television tear one another apart. Neither do I relish listening to college students claim victim status when it is not deserved. Is this in the service of our community? In 2019, victim status has taken on a new meaning. I believe it is necessary to confront undeserved victimhood in 2020 for what it truly is: a power play. As children, we cried to get what we wanted. As adolescents, we begged and pleaded for attention. As college students, we claim to be victims. It was once a liberal strategy to gain power. Now, both parties use the ploy. When I was laid off from my last job, I knew that I had to move out of state to continue working. I had to leave my friends and family, because the manufacturing jobs had left the state. I didn't cry "victim" of NAFTA and automotive market downturns; I posted to national job boards and moved myself to a different state. Then, I launched a new engine program with the help of my counterparts at my new company. I found a way to serve. Are we teaching our children to work hard, or are we teaching them to use anti-social behavior to gain an advantage over their peers?

CHAPTER 4
To Revert or Be Redeemed

Everyone has made mistakes in their life. Everyone has had terrible things happen to them. How did you react to those low moments in your life? Did you start over? Did you get help from friends, family, or your government? There is a rainbow after the storm. It's the storm that makes you stronger.

I was laid off three times in my career. Each time, my world was blown apart. Yes, I took social security twice in my life. Of my 30 years in the workforce, I was only out of work for one year. I know I made bad choices, but I never gave up on my dreams of getting married and raising my own family. When I was at my lowest, I found a church group and spoke about my issues to new friends. From those honest moments came close and personal friendships. I finally found the love of my life when I turned 39 years young. One of the men from that church group was the best man at my wedding.

I am not against social security for those who worked and were laid off. I'm not against social services for those who cannot work. What I am against are those who work the system to gain government benefits when they could be working. Living on the dole was once a dishonor. The Great Depression required a bootstraps answer, and FDR gave us work programs and social service handouts. The programs were supposed to be temporary until we got back on our feet back. Funny how the work programs ended but social security continues to this day. That's right; your ancestors hated being dependent on the government. They wanted to earn it and deserve it. They knew that, if they took the handouts, they would become a slave to the government.

A victim would say, "I can't control my situation. There are roadblocks and barriers." Well, few can change their life overnight. You need a plan. You need to know your strengths and work on them. You are needed, and you are wanted. If you open your heart and let in the love of your community, there is nothing you cannot accomplish. Each moment is a gift that you can use to turn your life around. Number your days, so you may gain a heart of wisdom. Plan your free moments and use them to better yourself. If you don't know what you are doing, ask questions from those you admire most. Seek out and strive for what is good. If you love your enemies and pray for those who persecute you, hearts will change, and doors will open. Believe me.

It happened to me. I was self-centered. I would search for what I could get rather than what I could offer. I would seek to be served rather than to serve. There are so many needs in this world. There are so many lonely hearts seeking love. Listen to Sting's famous song, "If You Love Somebody Set Them Free." That's what I want for all of us; I want to set the world free—for freedom and capitalism have been the strongest forces for good so far in our world's history. Globalism, paired with socialism, will only enslave our population for the benefit of the few. By pandering to our weaknesses, the Progressive left wants to hook you and make you compliant. Do you think we have a large wage gap now? Remember how the DNC was apologizing for the slow recovery in 2010? Remember how long it took to get back on our feet? Remember how our businesses were moving to Mexico and China due to the poor business climate here in the U.S. in 2015? Those were Progressive left choices. Have you noticed a booming economy since Trump took office and removed tons of regulations and red tape? This economy is great. I know my employer is hiring. The Progressive Democrats keep talking about a looming recession. Of course they are. That's the only way they might win back the presidency.

The standard of living in the entire world has risen since the beginning of the industrial revolution, according to the Economic History Association. The United States has the highest Gross Domestic Product in the world and the third highest growth rate since 1820. Your life is easier than your great grandparent's life. You have air conditioning, fuel-efficient vehicles, administrative jobs, and more choices at the grocery store than in any other country in the world. I have travelled Europe and the Far East. I feel there is more freedom here in the United States than anywhere else in the world. So, take heart and get moving forward!

In John 5:6, Jesus asked a sick man in Bethesda, "Do you want to be made well?" He had to ask this since many of us come to identify with our sicknesses. Many of us would rather stay in our current condition than seek help or healing to improve upon our situation. To that I say, get up, stand up, and join in the dance of life. Make your way and have your say. Shine your light to the world, and let everyone see how special you really are!

CHAPTER 5

Power and Responsibility

Like Stan Lee once said, "With great power comes great responsibility." Our elected representatives have been charged with carrying out the wishes of the voters. That's you and me. In a democracy, the power is supposed to rest in the hands of the people. Power is not to be used lightly. Your power is not a weapon used to tear each other down, is it? No, of course not. We are not here to create chaos. It is our responsibility to communicate our wants and needs to our representatives. It is also our responsibility to look beyond ourselves. A democracy is the most challenging form of government we know. It requires understanding, compromise, goodwill, and love of one another. The Founding Fathers bet their lives that the citizens can, as a whole, come up with better solutions than a monarchy. Right now, we need solutions. I'll be the first to admit that I don't have the answers. I do know that the citizens of the United States have given too much decision-making control to our representatives.

Words are powerful. We shape the world around us by what we say and do. I fully understand my responsibility to tell the truth while writing this book, as 1 Peter 3:10 says, "Whoever desires to love life and see good days, let him keep his tongue from evil and his lips from deceitful speech." Both the Republican Party and the Democratic Party have moved their ideologies to the extremes of acceptable political viewpoints over the past 30 years. Americans, too, have chosen opposite paths of acceptable speech, attitude, and viewpoints. To disagree with explanation and understanding of the others' viewpoint is our best model for behavior; to disagree with anger and without an open ear is the worst example of democratic behavior. Unfortunately, the commonest form of behavior I witness everyday is the latter.

As a Christian, I know that the Bible condemns lies and hate. Our ancestors knew that, but it seems we have forgotten. The liberal left feeds us lies in the Mueller report and in whistleblower reports. The far right speaks in absolutes and passes new immigration and trade policies without regard for the entire electorate. So much nonsense. On one hand, trade and protection are executive powers; on the other, immigration and trade ratification are within congress' powers. The media seems to only report the far-left agenda, like mockingbirds, repeating them over and over. It's a farce, it's slander, and it's unpatriotic. Though, the liberal left and the media claim the same of Trump and Fox News. The problem is that the DNC's claims are just words without proof. *How many false claims will it take before the American public will understand that the liberal left and the media are colluding? How many regulations must change without congressional involvement?*

Neither side is perfect. If the president tries to stop the way the media portrays him, the president takes away their First Amendment rights. If he gets angry, he's "unhinged." Face it; the media will never be on the Republican's side, because it is owned by those allied to the liberal left. Perhaps you don't care about that, but you should. Even a centrist Democrat like Tulsi Gabbard cannot escape the slander of the liberal left. This proves that certain democrats will eat their own to gain and retain power—and that's irresponsible.

Some of us have more capital and power than others. We hold sway over many with our corporation or association. Our team is strong, and our reach is vast. That's great. What are we doing with that power? Are we doing the most good for the most people? Or are we doing the most good for ourselves? Just look at the political landscape before us. Money funds political and cultural division. Division creates even more power, but for whom? It's the oldest trick in the books: divide and conquer. No one can buy the United States, but it seems like some are trying to. Special interest groups are one thing, but billionaires funding super PACs (political action committees) are too much. Luckily, there are too many homegrown, down-to-earth, rock-solid Americans for anyone to buy the United States. Those wanting to control the United States and drive us down the road of socialism wish to enslave us to the government. Those in corporations wish to get richer by making rules to suit their needs.

Once again, the powerful wish taxation without representation upon the masses. The deplorable people of America are smarter than you think. They know what the Progressives are doing, and they know what the rich are doing. It's not religion. It's not money. It's not racism. It's freedom that drives the people of the United States. It's freedom from internal tyranny of our own bloated government that drives Middle America to protest. The protests are just as fractured as the political parties are. At least there is some representation there. What is needed is good leadership to bring together the extreme viewpoints. I don't know how that can happen, but I know it needs to happen. I still remember Tip O'Neill and Ronald Reagan working together, begrudgingly, toward good legislation. Those times need to return. When I was a child, I watched my older siblings quarrel and fight with my parents and among each other. It was difficult to bear. For this reason, I prefer to promote peace and stability around me. I have always wanted my friends and family to come together in peace. It just makes life easier for everyone involved. Perhaps that's just too hopeful and innocent.

Did you know there are more than two million people on our nation's payroll? What if that group of people decided to control our government and rule this country? I am thankful for the service of our government workers. At the same time, I am distrustful of our bloated government, and I wish its staff would be trimmed down by at least 30 percent. Our government cannot be ruled by the unelected staffers. Our leaders were elected to serve the citizens of the United States.

The motto of Belhaven University in Jackson, Mississippi is "Not to be served but to serve." Our government needs to serve the American people again. We, as citizens, need to serve our fellow man once again. Slander and petty partisan politics need to be punished.

CHAPTER 6

Why Can't You Just Meet Me in the Middle?

There was a time when Congress legislated, the judicial branch ruled, and the executive branch needed congressional approval to wage war. That time is gone. We now have the judicial branch creating laws, presidents waging war and creating "policies," and Congress writing resolutions that do nothing but make noise. The 116th Congress has enacted only 56 laws this year, which equates to 1 percent of all legislation, but they have passed 282 resolutions. Resolutions accomplish nothing. I'll assume they passed resolutions in order to look busy. The president has changed so many regulations; I have no idea if the changes are good for the people or just good for corporations. Regulations are meant to protect citizens, corporate workers, corporate customers, and the environment. I understand the claim that regulations were replaced with less red tape. Yes, that is good for corporations who wish to do business in our country, but is it good for the citizens? How would we know?

Yes, it is the beginning of election season, but it seems like it is always election season. According to Govtrack statistics, in the election season of 2016, 3 percent (or 329 bills) of all proposed bills were signed into law. In 2012, only 2 percent of the proposed legislation was signed into law. Less legislation is acceptable for a short period of time—that's how the bicameral system was designed. No matter how much Barak Obama hated it, gridlock needs to be a part of government. However, we have deteriorating roads and bridges, antiquated gun screening laws, and trade deficits that need tending to. We need immigration reformation. We still have homeless on the streets in our major cities. China has growth on its mind. Instead of solving these problems, the Democrats in Congress only manufacture new problems and present left-wing agendas. Instead of talking quietly with the Democrats to resolve issues, Trump tweets up a storm. At least Trump is getting things done.

Russian collusion has proven to be a myth—the most publicized myth in all of American history. Wielding collusion seems to be a Democratic Party habit, based upon media coverage and security agency wrongdoing. What is the 116th Congress teaching our kids? They're teaching our kids to procrastinate doing homework. They're teaching that it's acceptable to lie on an epic scale. They're also teaching to double down on a lie when caught. I know you think it is Trump who is lying, but let's wait until the courts get involved. Then, I pray, we will find out the truth.

Lying is not a new thing in Washington, D.C. I doubt our country would have survived without some whopping ones. However, we are not living up to our potential as a world leader anymore. We have so much potential. We still have the biggest gross domestic product (GDP) of any country by far. *World Population Review* states that the U.S. had the highest GDP of $21.4 trillion in 2018, followed by China with $15.5 trillion and Japan with $5.4 trillion. So, our children are learning that wasting our potential is no big deal and blowing our nation's riches, like their allowance, can be tolerated. That's not how I was raised.

Our presidents have taken on more and more powers throughout the 20th century in order to complete the business of the United States of America. Without reform, I fear that Congress will become ineffectual as a system to check and balance our strong presidency. Without reform, I fear Congress will continue to form kangaroo courts—unauthorized, unofficial courts with the sole purpose of providing the illusion of a fair and legal process— and witch hunts like in the Salem witch trials. What a waste of taxpayer money! This country has lost its way. The court of public opinion and the biased media coverage have aligned with DNC-manufactured controversies to depose our current president. It hasn't worked, and it won't work. The precedent is concerning, though. The apathy and lack of public knowledge regarding the fake narratives is even more concerning. Due process and the rule of law have been replaced by deceit, hysteria, suspicion, and lack of evidence. These terms, Kangaroo court and witch hunt, describe exactly the current state of DNC activity against our president. At the very least, the perpetrators of these false and malicious investigations should be censured. The lack of evidence and hysteria brought forth by the media and the DNC on a daily basis cannot be understated. Just because something is repeated doesn't make it true. This is one source of the division in our political arena.

I prefer to discuss grace rather than division. The Who sang "Bargain" to show that one plus one doesn't equal one. Love brings people together in common causes. If we come together as one, compromise will be easier to commit to. Imagine how hard it is for you to sit across a table from me and tell me this book is not correct. It's much easier to do via email or a Facebook post, isn't it? We need our leaders to work together, in person, to hammer out good legislation. We have always had two separate factions. They will always fight our differences out in public. These past three years have been different, though. *Where is the love in our representatives?* I'm not looking for a hug-fest here. Talking to each other would be a good start. Working together for a common cause always strengthens a team. Our Congressmen can't even agree to the extent that Russia was involved in the 2016 election process. Power, money, and greed are the very things that brought down Rome and Greece. At this moment, we must make a choice. We are at the proverbial crossroads in our nation's history. This moment will define us. How we handle this partisan bickering scourge will set us on a path of healing or put us on the "eve of destruction." Will the gravy train keep running, or will we get greedy and try to hoard everything for one party or the other?

Segregation, like slavery, was about control of the poor population so that those in power could have a working class do the work for them. "King Cotton" was king only because the South had free labor to pick the cotton. The landlords of the South went to war to keep their economy going. It was the Democratic Party that fought to prolong slavery and segregation. You don't hear that discussed by the media. The backlash, after segregation, was so great that a Southern Democrat is hard to find these days. Segregation, by definition, is separation of disparate peoples. To conquer, you must first divide. It reminds me of the backlash against organized religion in Europe. After centuries of manipulation and lies, the corrupt church lost its sway over the population. Just like that, the American people can come to mistrust their representatives. I would like to tell my kids, someday, that our political leaders came to their senses, started talking, and formed new compromises. When I think of how hard our veterans fought for our country, I think we owe it to them to work together. The people will always have the vote, but we must use it wisely.

Both political parties come up with new ways to label us and put us into tidy, little groups. Separating people into smaller and smaller interest groups is a great way to divide and conquer. Do we want our kids to be segregated and distrustful of their neighbors? I don't. Love brings people together. Our Congress has lost its connection to the people and to the original intent of the Constitution.

Love seeks out the just and justice. The American people know a witch hunt when they see it—or, at least, so I thought. I have watched with eyes wide open and mouth agape as hatred and malice spewed from our nation's representatives. Sowing doubt and suspicion is not the work of good and just people. I believe the citizens of the United States see through these smoke screens and diversionary tactics. Perhaps the huge fundraising for Trump's reelection is a sign that the citizens know how unjust the government has become.

The government's injustice is most evident in the recent Russia investigation. Everyone knows you can indict a ham sandwich—at least, everyone *should* know that. Personally, I sat on a grand jury in the spring of 2019. I saw how easy it was to indict citizens. The original intent of a grand jury is to prevent the overreach of government into public affairs. The DNC investigators are currently being investigated as I write this book. The tables are turning, and I believe the truth will finally come out regarding the

DNC, media, and security agency collusion. Many of the bad actors have been driven from government positions. I can only hope that the American people will come to an understanding that you can't believe everything you hear; you need to check the facts behind the news stories. You need to find a new source of information when falsehoods are presented to you on a daily basis. It's too easy to point the finger at one person and demonize them.

I try to teach my kids a consistent level of justice and fair play for all. It's difficult for them to understand the many levels of justice in our country. I have a difficult time understanding it myself. Take, for instance, the difference between the investigation of the Biden family's dealings with Ukraine and China, which yielded no investigation at all, and the three-year constant probing of our current president. How is this fair? It isn't, and that's why Joe Biden's popularity has dropped in October 2019. I thank God for this little bit of justice. If it hadn't been for intelligent citizens listening, we may still have Joe Biden—a bought and paid-for candidate—running for president.

Now, we know that Russian collusion is like a visit from aliens—it never happened. Yet, I have not heard an apology from anyone proposing that narrative. I wait patiently as our Department of Justice rights itself and completes the counter investigations. I am thankful for the quiet search for the truth, courtesy of Bill Barr and his team. I hope to see bad actors indicted who sought to take down a sitting president. Our system is truly tarnished by this shakedown. Was it revenge for the treatment of Clinton during the Lewinsky scandal? Hardly a justifiable reason. The Bible teaches us that, when we take revenge, we are seeking to take His place. Do not seek to be God. Instead, seek out God's love and forgiveness. Our republic depends upon it. The only reason our republic exists is because of the goodwill of the people. If we lose our goodwill, we will lose our way of life.

CHAPTER 7
What is Love?

If you've been to a wedding in a church, you have probably heard the Bible verse from 1 Corinthians 13, which defines what love is. In this chapter, I want to discuss how politicians should act with love as opposed to how they are acting currently.

Love is kind, and kindness is allowing those you disagree with a chance to succeed. It's a choice you make to listen to those you disagree with. It's respectful to really think about the opposing viewpoint and to seek out common ground.

Love does not envy. If a president came from the American public and not from politics, why is this bad? Our president is a successful businessman; why is that bad? I want to tell my sons that they, too, can be president someday. I want to believe that, if someone has made a few minor mistakes in their past, they could still be president someday. Weaknesses need to be tested, and vetting must be completed. Many of my friends believe that presidents are handpicked before the primary voting begins. Based on the current Democratic race, I have to disagree. The primary voting, state to state, has replaced the contentious national conventions—and for good reason. The national conventions concentrated too much power in one place.

Love does not boast and is not proud. There is no way to run for president of the United States without boasting. There are different forms of boasting and pride, though. Should we vote for someone who takes pride in calling Americans deplorable? Should we vote for someone who uses slurs against the Jewish or Black Americans? President Trump certainly has pride in his abilities, but I don't see hate speech. I don't see him dividing our populace or creating division. I see him working hard to fix old problems and make our country new again. I have seen the crowds gather around Trump and have heard them use hate speech. Here is the opposite side of the problem in America: we are an immigrant nation. We must accept the new immigrant population into our country without bias. The Irish and Italian immigrants received opposition in the late 1800s—the Blacks ever since they arrived—and, unfortunately, hate speech will continue. You can't control an independent heart.

I see the Democrats being very concerned about speech and how it is used. Personally, I am tired of speech control. I side with Jordan Peterson on this account. He fought his own students and fellow faculty to keep his own free speech. In doing so, he galvanized the men of America and enraged the professors and the liberal left who wish to control you in any way possible. Dr. Peterson explains it this way:

> I've studied authoritarianism for a very long time—for 40 years—and [authoritarian governments are] started by people's attempts to control the ideological and linguistic territory. There is no way I'm going to use words made up by people who are doing that—not a chance.

Freedom of speech, just like the right to burn the flag, is a difficult freedom we must tolerate as citizens of a democracy. The left might as well start burning books and banning books, as they are already controlling your children's education in the public schools. Do you want your children to learn what LGBTQ+ means? Shouldn't there be an option to prevent your kids from attending that kind of biased cultural education? Since when did the minority control what the majority should learn?

Love is not rude and should never make people feel uncomfortable or unsafe. Our fine men and women of the military who place themselves in harm's way should be provided the ammunition and equipment necessary to complete their jobs, and they should receive proper medical treatment when they need it. The government is too big to properly handle one-on-one concerns between a doctor and a patient. Our military deserves our support both on and off the battlefield. If socialism brings the same medical service to everyone that the VA brings to our veterans, I will fight socialism until the day I die. Our veterans deserve the best medical service that money can buy. They shouldn't have to wait six months for their case to be heard. In some instances, they die before the VA agrees to treat them. The government should stay out of the medical business and stick to legislation. One government-issued Medicare card should be enough.

Love is not self-serving. Who is the DNC serving by attacking the president constantly? They are serving only themselves to regain power. Do you believe the president is self-serving? I see only evidence of hard work and creative ideas for improving our country. The majority of government staffers are pulled from states in the liberal left cultural region. This is unfair representation, since staffers serve alongside our elected representatives. They have too much opportunity to change the political landscape. Some staffers actually became angry and took revenge upon Trump after he chose not to hire them into his cabinet. Of course, there will be pushback from the opposition. Just because there is pushback should not dissuade a reformer from completing the job he has promised to do. As a candidate, Trump ran his campaign on "draining the swamp." He won the election. He has a mandate from the people. He needs to be allowed to reform the government. Based on recent polls, it looks like he will win by a large margin in 2020. I'm no soothsayer. An incumbent always has a better chance of winning.

Love is not easily angered and keeps no record of wrongs. Too often, our political parties remember past injustices and perpetuate anger between the classes. If we were truly one, why would our leaders separate us into factions? Factions can only divide. With these divisions come fighting within our nation. Our Constitution already reserves the right to free speech and freedom of assembly. This country is inclusive and should not be divisive. This country does not need the rhetoric of division and must reject it.

Shouldn't we support each other with love and give our children that example? Do we trust our current Congress to meet our needs as citizens? Seen from the lens of a family, or from that of a child, this country needs a change. I am dismayed by the infighting and think we need reformation from the inside out.

CHAPTER 8

We Are One

Our astronauts talk about it all the time. They saw the Earth from the Moon and realized that everyone they had ever loved lives on that planet. Can you imagine closing one eye and covering the distant Earth with your thumb? If you could just see the majesty of the Earth from the point of view of the Moon, you might just decide that God is real. What religion does is tie us to a higher cause. In binding us to higher aspirations, we are tied to each other. For better or for worse, we live on the same planet. We drink the same water and breathe the same air. We are one, whether you like it or not.

Marvin Gaye expressed sorrow for the war-torn world in his song, "Mercy, Mercy Me" to help us see that division only causes strife. War is not the answer. Only love can conquer hate. We've got to find a way to bring some lovin' here today. I wish all Americans would listen to Marvin Gaye's music again. Yes, he was a flawed man, but great love comes from the most unexpected places. Anger and hatred of different viewpoints is not the way to achieve a more perfect union. Listening and understanding each other is the only way to do so.

This might make me a dreamer. The difference between my dream and other dreams is that I support the American Dream. What's the American Dream, you ask? The opportunity we have to better ourselves and our station in the community. The ability to run for office or start a new business. The chance we have to rise above our meager existence and become president of the United States. There was a time when a small town lawyer could do it by himself. How can this country return to a place where morality, virtue, and grace are the factors by which our presidents are chosen? The same question could be posed for congressional seats. So, is it even possible to return our body politic back to Lincoln's time? With the increase in computer technology, many companies have downsized their administrative workforce to become more efficient. The government, on the other hand, has increased in size. Power is the reason for government growth. Everybody wants to rule the world. What if the power of computers were used to shrink the size of government? Can't those Harvard and Yale graduates work smarter, not harder? Go Blue. I wonder if the American Dream can survive another Page-Strzok-Steele debacle. What is the solution? It's an open-ended question that requires all of us to answer—to vote. Perhaps your vote in 2020 will be part of the solution.

Recently, I attended a Rotary Club meeting at which the Mississippi Civil Rights museum curator was speaking. He understood the need to bring to light the injustices and the separations of the past. By seeing the way we have failed in the past, we can better understand what is wrong today. Visitors to the civil rights museum can see the struggle, the pain, and the fear that gripped the state of Mississippi from its very beginning. Visitors learn that enduring pain and struggle will bring out the best in people. The music of Mississippi expresses the excruciating pain and suffering put upon the people. It also expresses the deep culture created by shared suffering and endurance. We must shed light on the current division in our government. We must see the truth behind the lies. It is our duty and our right to control our government and not allow it to control us.

CHAPTER 9

Don't Be a Parrot

To the youth in our universities, the powerful are taking advantage of your lack of experience in the real world. Without knowledge of the past, how can you judge the present with any amount of intelligence? Without working within corporations, how can you judge them? Without travelling around the world, how can you truly understand the real problems the world is facing? Most universities have been teaching liberal points of view since the '80s. Make up your own minds and express your point of view without shame or fear.

Be more than a follower. Do not parrot the far left or the far right. Protest those who want to use you. Ask questions of those who try to lead you at your university. Where is the money coming from? Why do you ask me to do this? What is the ultimate purpose and direction you want me to go in? In 10 years, you might find yourself asking how you got where you are, if you follow the leader blindly. Don't be a shill, don't be a pawn, and don't be a road for others to trample on.

The gift of free speech should be protected at all costs. Although, free speech is a double-edged sword. I enjoy listening to and laughing with every comedian I have ever heard. I may not agree with their politics, but the contrasts and hypocrisies they uncover are genius. I celebrate knowledge and understanding. I hope you do, too. To truly understand someone, you must listen deeply and put yourself in their shoes. Our world is full of attitude and ideas. So often, we are ships passing in the night. We sail on through our own worlds we have created. We keep to ourselves rather than engage in each others' points of view. I want to engage and grow from engagements in discourse, not sit in silent disagreement. I want to learn and grow in wisdom from the learning.

Don't you want to grow in knowledge and understanding? Do you think you know everything? Sorry, but no one knows everything. That's the failure of the so-called elites; they forget that they need others to succeed. All of us have weaknesses or blind spots. Even university professors know that they need help to solve problems outside of their field of knowledge. Mike Rowe, Discovery Channel's *Dirty Jobs* star, knows this best. He sees the hands-on workers dealing with the ugliest jobs and making the best of it. The working class and blue-collar types are needed and will never be replaced. Manufacturing jobs will always require a human touch to adjust, control, and prevent quality spills. Trash removal, water treatment, building maintenance, and plumbing are all honorable industries. Not everyone is a genius. Not everyone has excellent educational training that universities provide. We shouldn't denigrate the hands-on segment of our community just because they have less educational opportunities or capabilities.

Universities are a wonderful place to research all sorts of ideas and ideals. Even if you are not interested in college, you can still learn! Pick up a book and read or go online! Those with higher education have a duty to our community. As Plato put it, the highest goal in all of education is the knowledge of the Good. That is, not merely an awareness of particular benefits and pleasures, but acquaintance with the Form itself. The forms are truth, beauty, equality, and the Good. Plato would not endorse a leader who denigrates the hands-on segment of our community.

CHAPTER 10
Polarization

This land is not your land or my land. Our Founding Fathers warned us of a strong centralized government. Now, we have it. Money rules this country. The politicians pander to the poor. The rich get richer. So, what's new? Polarization of our parties has spread to the media, to Hollywood, and to you and me. We need peace—now more than ever. We need common decency to return to our relationships, our entertainment industry, and our halls of power. To do that, each of us needs to demand that our representatives work together to compromise.

I've attempted to discuss politics with those of all ideologies, but, to have serious discussion and compromise, we must respect each other's viewpoints and demonstrate respect for our counterparts. I'm not seeing respect in politics or in the media that I saw only 10 years ago, and I am not seeing respect in the streets of America that I saw just five years ago, either. I never saw the media attack President Obama. It's not because he was the perfect president—far from it. Antifa, a radical left movement, raised political protest to a contact sport over the past five years. The Trump rallies often go overboard when shouting, "Lock her up." Perhaps Hillary Clinton deserves it, but that's for the courts to decide.

CHAPTER 11

Obstacles and Temptation

As a society, we place so many obstacles in the path of our youth. We tempt them to buy with credit, making them a slave to the lender. We offer them sex on the internet, skewing their morality, and tempting them to have children before marriage. Alcohol and drugs, the perennial temptations, also lead them away from achieving the American Dream. There is no way to prevent these obstacles from interfering with our children, but we can educate our children and give them guidance, tools, and understanding to combat them.

However, public schools are not the places to teach morals and values—homes and churches are. Home is the place where children can receive the values and morals to recognize life's temptations, but religion is the strongest supporter and teacher in children's lives. Despite this, many families do not have the time to discuss morality with their kids each week. Some questions your children may have include should I follow my friends and take drugs, should I tell someone that I feel depressed, and how do I respond to peer pressure? Your children may not even know what to ask. Let them go to church and make up their own minds.

Perhaps organized religion is distasteful to you. Whatever the reason why you are against sending your children to church, I beg you to understand the important role religion plays in our world today. Without it, we are more likely to succumb to temptations, and our nation will grow towards corruption. Give children a chance to learn morals and values from religion before the world begins to tempt them. If you are irreligious, at least read and explain the teachings of philosophers—those from both liberals and conservatives. It seems to me that each generation is just a little smarter than the last, so I hope that we can re-implement morals and values into our lives. You never know how far your daughter or son will go. Sexual acts are a choice. We have, or should have, self-control. Give them the tools and knowledge they need before they leave your house. Love demands closeness and intimacy. Love, not sex, requires emotional bonds. Love is kind and not overbearing. For God's sake, talk to your kids, because we have a suicide problem in this country. A caring family is the best solution.

Our children need religion to overcome temptation, but they also need it to face dangers. In schools throughout the country, children are running scared and don't have a choice. They are begging for security, but there is no amount of security we can give them that will be enough. The government, in this case, has been, and will be, powerless. Rather than rely on our inefficient government, we should train and equip certain teachers to use and store a gun in a locker on school premises. We should give our teachers a fighting chance. Adding security guards in schools is a good move, but the selection of the security guards seems weak at this time. My cousin, a former police officer, is now a security guard at a school. It seems wise to employ a well-trained and well-vetted former military or police officer as a school security guard; those with proven experience will not shy away from a fight to protect our children.

CHAPTER 12

Cell Phones—the Newest Temptation

The technology you have in your hand can launch you in any direction. With it, you can start a business, communicate with your contacts, and keep a network of friends. You can schedule your day in order to fit in the things that really matter to you, such as volunteering. So, with all their potential, why are cell phones so frequently used to perform the most immoral acts? I'm talking about internet trolls. I'm talking about boasting tweets about your entire day. Committing immoral acts is a decision; it is a conscious choice you make. An independent mind is impossible to control, but a well-trained and moral mind can be reasoned with.

Do you find yourself, as a mother or father, fighting with your children over a cell phone? What you are fighting for, to a certain degree, is control over the path your children take. I'm shocked when I see an eight-year-old walk around with a smartphone. They are learning things no eight-year-old needs to learn. Is safety the reason we give our children smartphones, or is it something else? Do our children use them to call us or to play games and avoid learning?

How do we council our teenagers, though, in the proper use of their phones? This is where church groups for teenagers come in. We know that teenagers will push away from their parents. Perhaps it does take a village to raise a child—a Christian village with correct moral teachings. Sometimes, I think everyone needs some guidance to determine when to get your face out of the smartphone and reconnect with your loved ones.

Social networks are the new wonders of our world, but they can also lead us down the wrong paths. I suppose the sheer idea of connecting to like-minded people draws us in. There's nothing wrong with kibitzing with a fellow guitar player or fellow competitive soccer player on the internet. The danger comes when we gain a level of holier-than-thou attitude, because there is always a group to back up our point of view—however wrong it may be—online. The collaboration that small groups bring can be beneficial, but we need to worry about groupthink, which is a "psychological phenomenon in which the desire for harmony or conformity in the group results in an irrational or dysfunctional decision-making outcome" ("Groupthink," *Wikipedia*).

The truth within a group is not necessarily the truth of the entire country. Just as a sample of data cannot represent the whole data, small collaborative groups can only be trusted based upon the diversity of the population inside that group. Small group points of view can be easily manipulated. They can provide a path toward oppression of their neighbor since the small group has more power than an individual. Everybody wants to feel special. Everybody wants more stuff or more power. It's been the same for generations: we want. A Christian knows that God wants the best for us. What He wants for you may not be what you want for yourself. God opposes the proud but gives grace to the humble.

This world is not just about winning. It's about lifting each other up. If Elon Musk wanted to buy the Bahamas, he could have. Instead, he created the newest successful auto company in the world that makes green electric vehicles. *Wow!* At the same time, he created SpaceX to lift us up into the heavens and possibly save the human race from future extinction. This man deserves our support. That's what life is all about: solving a problem and lifting each other up. Do I do it, too? Yes, I do. I volunteer, perform in a worship band, and coach and train our youth. Whom do you support and why? If you explained your reasons to a group of 1,000 people, would it hold up? Would you be cheered by the crowd or booed off the stage? It's impossible to be everything to everybody. Be the best you. That's all anyone can ask of you.

CHAPTER 13

Sex Politicized

For too long, we have allowed our friends and relatives to remain in domineering relationships. Whether it be a business relationship, political relationship, personal relationship, or any other relationship, we owe it to our neighbors and loved ones to prevent violence and domineering behavior from persisting. Rather, friendly competition and mutual respect—collaboration and compromise—should be promoted in all relationships. Perhaps the Me Too movement can be used as a blueprint for how the U.S. Congress should communicate with each other. Domineering attitudes from either party need to be shut down.

When I was 28 years old, I realized that I needed to put the same effort into a relationship that I put into my daily job. It was a turning point for me. Before, I was sitting back in an easy chair, metaphorically speaking, in my relationships. Now, I was finally listening to my partners. I was not a domineering male, and I had seen the changes in our culture and was adapting to them. I wouldn't call it being "woke"; I would call it setting a new course toward a shared and loving relationship. Congress needs to adapt to our new internet-based world just like men born in the '70s had to adapt to a new set of moral and cultural rules. A truce is needed to extend an olive branch to the executive branch. The impeachment talk is just bluster without proof. That type of accusation without proof is just as domineering as any misogynistic male supervisor of the 1960s. The DNC needs to step back from this abusive path.

I suppose the backlash against white men comes directly from our overbearing fathers and grandfathers. I have witnessed the change in my family firsthand. My family had the breadwinner, my father, and nurturer, my mother. That's how society worked for thousands of years.

My mother has played the organ at church for 70 years; my sisters have held excellent jobs for most of their working lives. The emergence of women in the workforce since World War II changed the political and cultural landscape of our country like no other historical event. We have always had powerful, beautiful, and smart women, but accepting women in the workplace has been a slow process. I know many who have pushed against the glass ceiling with disgust and impatience. We are not living in the '80s anymore; women have taken on leadership roles in most major industries: Mary Barra is the CEO of General Motors, Indra Nooyi was the CEO of Pepsico, Ginni Rometty is the CEO at IBM, and Marillyn Hewson is the CEO of Lockheed Martin. And the beat goes on (The Whispers).

Culturally and morally speaking, men and women should be given the same rights and privileges given to them by law and the Constitution. However, I'm not saying that everything is equal in business, and I'm not saying that everything should be equal in business. Women also have a duty to nurture their children. Men, too, must have a role in that. There was a time when middle class families could have a working parent and a stay-at-home parent. Those days are gone. Taxes and cost of living are too high. Dual-income families are the new normal, and legislation and corporate rules need to keep up with that trend.

I hope you are not shocked that an older white male like me could be pro equal rights for women, minorities, etc. I never had to prove myself to others until I turned about 28 years old. White males may get some privilege as youth, but we get no special treatment as adults. I feel the condescending eye upon me as an older white male. Younger people think I am out of touch with the younger crowd. I probably am, since I work 50 hours a week. I'm not complaining; I just want to debunk this "privilege" crap. Why are we still blaming our current situation on the rule of males in the workforce? My family knows about domineering fathers. My family has overcome our past. We can now express our love in public. We can share in the Christian brotherhood and sisterhood that is spelled out in detail in the Bible. Identity politics is the worst form of division perpetrated on our culture. It has no place in our society. If this is the vision of the liberal left for the 2020 election, then let's call it 2020 DiVision.

CHAPTER 14

A Fatherless Society?

Yes, our cultural rules have changed since 1980. I think they have changed for the better, although I do feel that white males are marginalized more and more. Distrust of how white males treat others around them, perhaps earned in the '80s and earlier, continues to this day. On the other hand, have we gone too far? Nurturing and loving fathers are somehow discounted today. Fathers have less authority over their daughters. The media tells our young girls to revolt and separate from their families too soon. Social media has pulled our children's focus away from parental guidance and toward more shallow pursuits.

So, do we want to replace our father figures in this culture? Sometimes, I feel that we do. I hear the emotional cries of the left screaming out against males, especially older males. I also hear cries for socialism. Are we trying to replace the father's role with an overbearing government? Is the far left seeking to become our father figure? What's going on? Don't you know there are men out there with love in their hearts just waiting to be your hero? I see them at the soccer field. I see them in police uniforms. I see them on the basketball courts. I find them at church and at schools. They are everyday heroes. Not so flashy. Not as super as you might want—more the flabby type—but still able to lift you up higher than an eagle.

Let's not choose a new overlord or tyrant for our government. Our nation was formed, and was successful, because it was a nation *for* the people, *of* the people, and *by* the people. Big government doesn't care about you. Big government just wants to get bigger, more powerful, more overbearing, and more controlling. Let's not create a bigger problem. Let's start trusting the gentlemen standing next to you.

Government can be small and still keep a safety net for its citizens. Turn some of those "intelligence agencies" into social welfare agencies. Have them serve the people for once.

CHAPTER 15

Morality of the Unborn

This is a touchy subject. I am a Christian, so I think you already know which side I am on here. Please at least read this chapter rather than skip over it. At least understand why this country needs to take two steps back, in my humble opinion.

I have friends aching to adopt; they are begging for help. At the same time, I see young Americans who don't want a pregnancy and decide to abort the fetus. The temptation for teenage and pre-marital sex is great, and the desire to avoid pain is as well. We seem to want the easy way out—never mind the rest of your community that is willing to adopt your healthy, unborn child.

Pregnancy puts unwanted shame on a young mother. Giving up a child places heartache on her. I understand the decision-making process, but I don't agree with it. Once again, our society and culture are failing to protect human life. We seem to throw away the precious opportunity to give life in the rush to avoid pain. This is a decision. No one wants to talk about that. A father and a mother chose to have sex without protection. The political parties want to pander to the poor, young mother. It takes two to tango. No one is completely at fault in every situation. To follow a wrong with another wrong—well, that doesn't make it right.

As a foster father, I have seen adoptive opportunities lost due to a life-or-death decision made by the birth mother. It always comes down to a decision. Many adoptive parents are willing to pay for hospital costs, third trimester home care, and even after birth care for the birth mother. Why is it that, when a controversial issue arises, we find a way to choose the path of least pain? Sure, you are giving the poor woman funds to have an abortion, for whatever reason, but, at the same time, you are funding the death of a newborn. Abortion is immoral in Christian teaching. Never mind what the government does. What are *you* doing about it?

We are the creators of children. We are the ultimate power over the unborn child. We play God, and some of us play a terrible God while others play the most beautiful one.

Here is a thought experiment I came up with the other day. Say you were sitting at a table with five other adults and one of them was dying of cancer. That one person has a chance to live. Now, stay with me here, what if you somehow had control over whether that person lives or dies? Your choice would depend upon how ashamed you are. The amount of shame is more than you think you can bear. The pain you are feeling is more important to you, somehow, than the chance for life that the cancerous person has. You chose to take away their chance for life so that your pain and shame will be less—just like many mothers do with their unborn children. Those at the table can see you do this. You know that they know you've chosen to condemn this other person to death. Your shame takes on a whole greater level of pain due to the escaped knowledge. Somehow, you cannot control that the knowledge is out there. Would you take back your decision based on that lack of control? Does it truly matter whether someone else knows your decision? What if that table had been located in a room of 600 people, and all of them knew your choice? Would your decision change?

Now, suppose that you are sitting at the table of six and the person you have power over is your unborn child. You chose to have an abortion, and everyone at the table knows your choice. In fact, everyone in the *room* knows your choice. Will you carry your child to term because everyone knows or because you think it's the right thing to do? Will you go through with the abortion, knowing that you are condemning your unborn child to death? Does the crowd have any effect on your decision?

A decision is yours to make, and it can be changed up to the moment you take action. Truth cannot be changed, and it cannot be coerced or manipulated. Truth is unmoving and permanent. Truth is absolute and no amount of legislation can affect it. Truth does not depend upon how many people know your choice. This truth is that a chance for life is within you. What will you do? Whether or not you feel the pain and shame of rape, the unborn child does not know. Your children have no knowledge of how they were conceived. Many in our culture discount this child's chance for life, because they believe they have sole control over their body in this instance. This, however, is a weak argument, because you are taking only your own viewpoint into consideration and not the viewpoint of the community. Strength in a community comes not only from the size of the community but also the morality of it. A chance for life, small as it may seem, is still life. To take away any being's life must be justified by something more than pain, suffering, and shame. Only the loss of the life of the pregnant mother could possibly outweigh such an opportunity for human life.

Forget government intervention. Forget what your friends or family say. What I am talking about is intrinsic truth. No amount of anguish can possibly outweigh the chance for life. Life is a gift we have been given by our mother and father. How can we deny it to another? The culture of abortion lacks truth and beauty. I cannot sing a song that would honor the act. This is why the Christian church denies the right to abortion. I believe it needs to be said, once again. Our cultural values have swung, as a pendulum, away from intrinsic truth toward some distorted view of right and wrong. Pandering to a mother's choice to abort a fetus leads us toward active euthanasia. In one case, we are terminating the life of the infirm (chance for life in a limited fashion), and, in the other, we are terminating the chance for life of the unborn. Both are horrific choices. The unborn is not infirm, though. Abortion affects more than just the mother and her morality; the community has lost something, too.

CHAPTER 16
Adoption as a Lifeline

I have also been an adoptive father, receiving the gift of two sons and the birth of a third. No amount of shame or pain can possibly last after receiving, for the first time, a newborn or adopted child. This is why we must rethink our cultural choices. There are ready and willing parents out there wanting children to raise. I was one of them. There are intelligent and good people who desire the chance to raise a child in a good home. How can we deny their opportunity? They wait as we sit and take no action. College students, here is your higher calling. Fight for this worthy cause.

I understand your outcry. *How could you demean the anguish and the hurt that is suffered by women during a brutal attack?* It's true that I've never been brutally attacked. I've never been to war, and I've never given birth. I have witnessed the pain, though, and the lifelong suffering of those who cannot hide from their skin color and their heritage of slavery. Just as the beautiful music comes from terrible beginnings in Mississippi, so, too, can a beautiful life, if you let it. When you reach my age, you might wonder what that child would be like now. You could have found out, if you had let them live—if you'd braved the hurt and the shame. If you'd given yourself away for the sake of another. If you'd let your child live.

This country was formed under the barrage of gunfire. The soldiers, though just boys and untrained men, would not relent to pure force of will. Bravery and sacrifice were on full display when, under unrelenting barrage, our flag was held high by the men of Fort McHenry. Francis Scott Key wrote his famous song, "The Star-spangled Banner," not because the flag was flying high by chance. No, the soldiers of the Fort gave their lives to physically hold the flag high as they were slaughtered under cannon fire. That's the kind of sacrifice that has made the United States of America great. Sacrifice for unrestrained belief in a higher power. Sacrifice for higher aspirations than the old world could provide. Sacrifice for their family and the capitalistic promise for a greater future.

CHAPTER 17

Fair and Impartial Criticism

While we wage cultural warfare, our friends in the East have been capitalizing on our weakness. Are we sowing the seeds of love, or are we sowing the seeds of destruction? Can we come together soon enough to shut down a second cold war? Yes, China is now second in the world in terms of gross domestic product. They also hold some very large loans provided to the United States of America to service our national debt. How can we criticize our president for trying to right our governmental ship? Our trade deficits made our country weak, our debt has mortgaged our future, and our Department of Justice has been turned upside down with activist judges.

Previous administrations have allowed ISIS a foothold in the Middle East, and they have allowed China a foothold in the South China Sea. How could they allow these obviously offensive and dangerous acts to occur? The previous administrations say they are for globalism, but all they were really doing was weakening the United States foreign policy by allowing China and Syria to act boldly. They say they were helping the United States recover, but, really, they were giving away billions of dollars in bad trade deals and the poorly laid out Paris Agreement. The previous administrations also claimed to be supporting the financial recovery, yet the EPA and IRS regulations weighed heavily on our fine corporate institutions.

It's only fair to criticize just the same as the media criticizes the Republican presidents. Justice is blind. Shouldn't our criticism of presidents' actions also be blind to political leanings? Love is blind when we feel the euphoria of new love and don't really know our new partner yet. Similarly, justice should be blind, since we don't understand all of the concerns of our political adversaries. I never heard the mainstream media express discontent with the Obama administration. How easy it is to lead when the media tells you how great you are. Barak Obama used the power of the presidency to the same degree, or more, than our current president, Donald J. Trump. To impeach a sitting president for perceived power grabs isn't truth. Let's remember the actions taken by Obama, which had far worse repercussions than those taken by Trump. The Cato Institute and Garrett Epps reported that the following exploits that occurred during the Obama administration underwent criticism:

1. The 2011 Libya intervention without authorization
2. James Clapper lying to Congress about domestic surveillance
3. Aggressive posture toward journalists
4. Obamacare being deemed unconstitutional
5. The Dodd–Frank Wall Street Reform and Consumer Protection Act
6. The Chrysler bailout
7. Political profiling by the IRS
8. Recess appointments
9. DACA and DAPA allowing illegal immigration
10. Letter sent to University of Montana urging the crackdown on unwelcome speech
11. Clean Power Plan (EPA sites Section 111 as a permit for the federal government to regulate existing sources of pollutants already regulated under section 112)

These actions and so many more ignored the bounds of separation of powers and federalism written in the Constitution. Yet, the 116th Congress has decided to hold impeachment hearings against President Trump for his investigation into the Biden family. The president is the "top cop" of our country. He must be allowed to do his job without the threat of impeachment.

I call this "Divide":

> We multiply
> We Divide
> Got to simplify
> There is no side
>
> There's only one
> There's only us
> Dividing our sons
> Losing our trust
>
> Can we look away?
> Can we do better?
> Money's sway
> Pride so tattered.
>
> We've got love
> Let us last longer
> Use that power
> Make our world stronger!
>
> Live like no other
> Rain falling
> Be a good brother
> Find your calling.
>
> 'Cause all God wants is you.
> You.
> It's you
> All God wants is you!

Not only do we have enemies to fight outside of our borders, but we also have internal challenges. We have immigrants, both legal and illegal, that were poorly vetted. The results are a multitude of bad actors within our borders who wish to do this country harm. Our government has been tasked to ensure domestic tranquility, but, instead, were are getting far-left and far-right factions that squabble instead of finding common ground.

Our country is strongest when we have a common goal or a common enemy. I urge our country's leaders to come together to fight for freedom, for love, for our fellow man across the globe, and to not fall into the mire of fractured and ugly politics. Yes, I know it is an election year. Can we not put our best foot forward for once? Can we not debate the issues with clear strategies to help the American people? Please, don't allow another election of 1860. In 1860, the United States was divided over states' rights and the use of slavery in the south. The South seceded after losing the election. The South, concerned about losing the free labor of its slaves, had to secede in order to preserve its power. While our country is not in danger of secession, it is in danger of losing freedoms to a domineering socialist government.

CHAPTER 18

Hard Work and Focus

There are job opportunities, even in the worst times here in the United States. It takes hard work and focus to find them. There is no excuse for a lack of hard work. It's a decision, and it is a form of sacrifice. If you want to succeed, the United States is the easiest place in the world to do so. This is why you see people moving here from all over the world. The United States will always attract immigrants as long as we keep our values and our form of government. We need to compete as a country to make our environment the most appealing to corporations. Running this country like a business is essential in our new political environment.

In the '60s, there was a reason to protest racism, sexism, and war. Back then, segregation still had a hold on our country. Back then, women could not make a living wage and were kept out of the workforce. Life is good today. Jobs are plentiful. There is no segregation. Many of my working counterparts are Black. Many of my working counterparts are women. Perhaps we have further to go, but that's no reason to demonize a sitting president.

It's funny how the millennial generation is doing their best to avoid hard work and sacrifice. You can have your tiny houses and your super saver life hacks, but you don't need to live in a 200 square foot home to save money; you just need to invest in your 401(K) and save until you retire. If you focus and work hard, you can reach the American Dream easier now than ever before.

I have seen many Millennials retire at a very young age. There's a wide world out there that needs your skills and experience. You could start your own business and set up passive income streams for yourself and your family. You could feed the hungry with missionary work. You could teach people to read. You could even bring clean water to those in need. There is more to life than driving a Corvette while in debt up to your gills. I teach my kids to save their money and pay for items with cash; I wish our government and our citizens would do the same. When you reach working age, remember these words: Dave Ramsey's seven baby steps. Look it up. Thank you, Dave, for your service.

CHAPTER 19

Immigration

On the Statue of Liberty, there is a poem inscribed: "Give me your tired, your poor, / your huddled masses yearning to breathe free. / The wretched refuse of your teeming shore." A noble poem, to say the least. The United States of America was formed as hope to the world. We are still looked up to for political and economic guidance. Yes, I think immigration should be reformed. I have no idea how, since it is a very deep topic. I have felt the pull of immigration debates for the past year. I agree with the need to accept a complete cross-section of the world as immigrants. I saw the tide of illegal immigrants across our southern border—the children used as means for an adult to enter. Dishonesty is not the way to start a new life. I don't want my kids to start their lives by lying and cheating. I hope you don't, either.

Immigrants have made this country strong. Almost everyone I know has immigrants in their family history. At the same time, we must balance the security and health of our citizens with the desire to help others. Again, this is not racism; this is common sense. Why can't Capitol Hill agree to allow the immigration of 50 percent professionals and 50 percent working class into our country as citizens? That seems like a wonderful compromise. I'm not an immigration expert, and this subject is way too deep for me to investigate. We don't want drug cartels shipping opioids and killer drugs to our youth. We don't want dangerous felons roaming our streets. For instance, fentanyl has shocked our society, leading to countless overdoses. Do we care about the wellbeing of our youth and college-aged kids? I do.

"There is neither Jew nor Gentile, neither slave nor free, nor is there male and female, for you are all one in Christ Jesus" (Galatians 3:28). The Jews were once foreigners in Egypt. Irish Americans and Italian Americans were once looked down upon by White Anglo Saxon Protestants only 100 years ago. We should not mistreat those who wish to enter the United States of America. Our future as a civilized nation depends upon how open our arms can be. Build the wall, but put some doors in it for those who love liberty.

CHAPTER 20

What is the Truth (and Can We Handle It)?

The truth, in this brave new world, is more difficult to find. In the past, we could look up the Webster's truth in the dictionary and be confident in it. Now, we read sources online and assume the message is biased. History is rewritten all too often. The truth is out there, but, to find it, you have to constantly compare the stories from multiple news sources and read between the lines. Not everyone has a connection and an inside source of information that they can trust.

The American voter has little time to search for what is best for our country. It is our country, though, and we must put forth effort to keep it strong. Too often, we only vote for what's best for ourselves. We let others tell us what is best. Instead, we should understand the positions of all parties and vote based on the common good. We desire what we want now with little regard for long-term effects. Instead, we should be voting for the long-term good of our country by approving some fair amount of tax until the deficit is paid off. You must make a choice and stand by it; don't be fooled when someone says it's a grey area. Right and wrong exist, and, if you read enough, you will know.

CHAPTER 21

The Hypnotized Never Lie

Have you repeated a TV news anchor's viewpoint recently? Talking heads and correspondents are paid to hook you in and keep you engaged. You may think you're following the opinions of those on the show, but you might actually be following some rich guy in his New York apartment. If you don't believe me, ask yourself who pays the bills for a news show. Advertising, of course—a business. Who owns the business? Some rich guy living in a New York apartment is one possibility. Do you think that guy wants to pay for a television news show that disagrees with his political viewpoint?

Who pays the talking heads? The network and the television show manager. Who owns those news channels and the television networks? All but one media outlet spouts out liberal and sometimes far-leftist points of view. Are they giving you the least painful point of view so that you keep watching? Is that the least painful direction, the best direction to go? You should know whom you are following, and you should be thinking, "Is this the best direction for my community? For my children?"

Perhaps the shows you are watching are pandering to what you want to hear. We all want a happy and loving community. We all want to live in a utopia. Each of us has an agenda or cultural norm we abide by, which we believe will get us close to a utopian world. No matter how much you think your utopia is what everyone else wants, you can't force your political viewpoint on others. That's egocentric. That's utopian socialism. For example, the liberal left wants to give you free college tuition, but they don't provide the cost and the taxes you will have to pay for the rest of your life. We must compromise with the rest of our community to reach a common ground. So, when you spout out some talking head's viewpoint, I hope you are testing their theories and checking the facts before you repeat them. I hope you are not running to your computer to tweet out your favorite quote of the night. Following a power-hungry party leader blindly is a great way to put into power somebody with the bad intentions and the right words. I wonder if the leaders of the DNC could stop this insane slander and go against their own party to end this division.

Segregation in our country was only finally defeated by President Johnson and President Kennedy. President Johnson, a Democrat, was very brave when he ended segregation—going against his own party's point of view. Johnson signed the Civil Rights Act on July 2, 1964, in honor of JFK. It was a very unpopular thing to do among his closest supporters. Some believe JFK lost his life due to his fight against segregation. It wasn't easy for them, and, if you give your freedom away, it may be a long time before this world has another chance to be free. Are you sure that the pandering from the far left will not just put you deeper into slavery? Single Americans pay 25.6 percent of their earnings in taxes (16th highest in the world), according to Amy Fontinelle of *Investopedia*. Married couples with two kids pay 13.6 percent of their income to Uncle Sam (21st highest in the world).

Socialism will only increase your tax bill. The rich aren't going to pay it. The rich use debt to hide their assets and avoid taxes. No, taxes still come out of the poor and middle class' paychecks. You think you are getting something for nothing? You think those great promises from the left won't hit your pocketbook. Dire Straits said it best in "Money for Nothing."

CHAPTER 22

A Higher Purpose

Do you agree with the Bill of Rights and the Constitution? Are those old documents not relevant enough for you as a young American? Those rights are the most precious of all rights ever given to a body of people in the history of our world! The right to a fair trial, the right to bear arms, the right to free speech, and the right to practice your religion without interference—how can anyone disagree with that? Thousands of people in Hong Kong would prefer the rights granted to them by the Bill of Rights and Constitution rather than those by an authoritarian state.

Recently, a late night talk show host asked citizens on the street to list two or more freedoms from the Bill of Rights. Sadly, they had trouble giving one. Apathy is the first step towards losing one's rights. You may not care, but there are millions all over the world that know the United States is the leader in freedom, and the U.S. is their dream place to live for that reason.

Let's protest for the higher cause. There will always be a winner and a loser in politics. Losing one election is not the end of the world. Stop protesting every little change. There is so much more to live for. Try giving your time and talent to those in need. Inspire others with great works of art or music. Travel to foreign lands and find out what sacrifice really means. Did you know that Roman and Israeli historians Cornelius Tacitus and Flavius Josephus, respectively, agree that Christ died on the cross? I think I can trust that to be a fact. My question is why did he choose to die on the cross?

Why did he choose pain and sacrifice? Shouldn't we take a cue from him and find our own cross to bear?

Let's find in ourselves a higher aspiration. It's hard to take the leap toward a new goal. It's a decision. It's the first step. It's that leap of faith. When you don't know the road ahead but start walking down it, you have taken a leap of faith.

Today, you can research before you leap. You can pick up that phone and search out your direction. Even that act is a step in the right direction. You just learned something new. Keep going. Keep learning. Keep growing in knowledge. Your children will see you and follow you to greater awareness and a greater future. Don't rely on the public school system to raise your children; that's not their job, and, from what I hear, the public school teachers are tired dealing with poorly raised kids. How can you expect your kids to learn when they won't even listen to you? We are not our children's buddies. We are their parents with all the responsibilities that go along with that. Ephesians 6:4 says, "Fathers, do not exasperate your children; instead, bring them up in the training and instruction of the Lord." OK, so maybe you think raising your child to believe in an invisible being who speaks to you in your head is the most insane thing ever. Ask yourself what is more beautiful than a God who laid down his life for you. In whose company would you rather be—that of a power-hungry group chanting and spewing hate speech and taking down everyone around them or that of a supportive group of believers who are patient, kind, loving, and respectful?

CHAPTER 23
To Search and to Strive

If the citizens of the United States were truly searching for truths, we would not have a problem today. You may think we just need to get that Trump guy out of office to eliminate the problem, but Trump is not the problem; he is the response to the problem. He is the embodiment of the American people's anger toward both the left and the right.

Stop the record. Yes, I just said he embodies anger toward both the left and the right—the conservatives and the liberals. If you remember, the Republican Party was not pleased to accept Donald Trump as their nominee back in 2015.

The far left has gone off the deep end with unsustainable plans to spend your money and put you even further in debt. Pandering is a new art form, but pandering is as old a practice as the city-state (read some Greek or Roman history, if you dare). Roman Emperor Constantine struggled to hold the empire together in the last few years of the Western empire's existence. He had to and pander to the barbarians. The citizens of Rome would not fight and were in political disarray. According to a new book, *Mortal Republic: How Rome Fell into Tyranny*, political messaging during the 2018 elections hinged on many of the same concerns expressed by the Romans when they turned to an emperor for stability rather than facing the unstable and degraded citizenry.

What am I talking about? Globalism. Your money was sent overseas for decades to prop up a favored nation. That was the predominant strategy for years. Our country basically paid off leaders of other countries to be our ally. Who do you think benefited the most from all of those favored nation status payoffs? Was it the common man on the street or the business owner who helped put that Republican or Democrat in office? Think of it this way: do you respect a kid at school who pays you to be his friend? Some see it as a perk; I see it as the fleecing of America.

What about Nationalism, you might ask? Some say it's racist at its heart. I agree that nationalism can be a road to racism. I also believe our country has been through both nationalistic and globalist eras. There is no proof that a nationalistic agenda will directly lead to racism. I find a nationalistic agenda can lead to greater patriotism. Remember patriotism? Remember love of country? What's wrong with that if taken in moderation? Middle America knows that we cannot save the world if our own house is not in order.

Does a business give away its trade secrets? No, but the United States does give away its best research and development to other countries. Why do we allow this to happen? If the United States wants to lead the world toward a better future, we need to first educate and elevate our own.

CHAPTER 24

Tax and Spend

Kindness and helping hands are necessary until people are back on their feet. I support many of our safety nets for the poor. At the same time, the United States is not a free ride. We cannot support someone indefinitely, unless they are incapable of working due to illness, either mental or physical. The road toward socialism is a downhill road, because it's so easy to say yes to free lunch and free college—free whatever. Once the money runs out, and it will when the corporations and the millionaires leave, then you have a very long uphill battle. You just gave away your future. Your greed got the best of you. Don't fall prey to the siren call of socialism. Stay true to the hard work of your ancestors. Learn to love one another once again.

As U2 would put it, "All I Want Is You." The Beatles would say, "All You Need Is Love." You don't need power. You don't need money. You need the checks and balances of the United States Constitution. You need to keep in check those who would steal your money and your freedom. Do you think the Constitution is just a set of old, quaint ideas? When the debt of the United States reached $15 trillion, meaning that my grandchildren cannot even finish paying it off, is that quaint? When people receive tax dollars when they don't need them, is that quaint? Did you know that taxation without representation was the reason that the United States was formed? Dumping tea into Boston Harbor was a direct protest against the King of England who wanted the colonies as slaves to pay for his foreign wars with France.

What does the United States Government use your tax dollars for? Do you know or even care? Why do we pay 50 percent or more of our earnings and purchases to the government? Does Congress truly represent the good of the people? Do the courts truly rule impartially? We can do better. We, as the citizens of the United States, seem too wrapped in our daily lives. We can vote for a change agent like Donald Trump, someone who turns a business around, but cannot explain to him what we want him to do!

What do you want for the United States? Do you care? I do. Do you want to form a more perfect union? I do. Do you want to see people come together and be as one? I do. Why do I want these things? Without them, our nation will descend into chaos of squabbling factions even more so than we are now. Is it the end of our nation? Of course not. Is it the end of the notion, "for the common good?" Perhaps it is. What's the alternative to our people sucking on the proverbial tit of the government welfare system? What's the alternative to spending on domestic and international defense?

How about we bring business sense back to the United States Government? Ruling by emotion hasn't worked. Ruling by the political elite has fallen short. We have the strongest economy in the world by far, yet we can't pay our bills? That's ridiculous.

CHAPTER 25

Trade Deficits and Policies

We gave away trade deficits to our neighbors and competitors for generations. Where did that get us? Ever since the Carter administration, this country has run a trade deficit with Japan, Europe, and China. President Reagan was the first to point this out. Normal trade, by definition, is an equal return for the value of goods and services. However, China has been dumping low-quality goods for so long—and our misguided corporations have been buying these low-quality goods for so long—that manufacturing in the United States went on life support.

I, personally, was tasked to send manufacturing work to China while I worked at Siemens in 2008. I worked at Ford Motor Company in 1996 while watching outsourcing of manufacturing to Mexico. NAFTA forced my friends to leave the automotive industry. I have fought to keep my job as others were laid off around me. I was forced to move out of the state of Michigan to find a manufacturing job. Even the Japanese automotive plants in the United States were ready to move business to Mexico and China at the end of the last administration. This is very personal to me, so I applaud the Trump administration for bringing manufacturing, the cornerstone of any country, back to the United States.

We had to compete against Europe and its strong trade partnership, and the cost of manufacturing in the United States was prohibitive at that time and under those circumstances, which spurred our need to globalize. Still, I understand that our regulations and our political climate were part of the problem. Look at how strong our economy and our stock market has been since the cuts in regulation under the Trump administration. What is the point of punishing our country's corporations? Okay, corporate greed and the destruction of our environment. That was 30 to 40 years ago. Today is a new day, and our corporations have paid back most of their debts to society. Why, then, were we hamstringing our businesses? I'm waiting for an answer, as I am not the captain of any industry.

Manufacturing provides the less educated with ready and available jobs. It gives our citizens a chance to succeed and live out the American dream. We need manufacturing in the United States. What else would all those immigrants do to better themselves and their families once they legally cross the border?

CHAPTER 26

Let's Compromise our Way to a More Perfect Union

"A union of disparate peoples from all over the globe will never work," said the rulers of Europe when the United States was first voted into being. The squabbling masses and the poorest from all over the world could never create a strong and enduring country. Who could have ever believed that we, from the mobs of early America, could become the noblest country in the history of our world?

Snobbery must be contagious, since that same high-browed attitude can be seen in the "Elites" here in the United States. I hear about university professors spouting liberal dogma. I see Hollywood and the mainstream media do the same. It's no wonder that the people of Middle America have voted for a change agent such as Donald Trump. We need change! The music from the far left is like a bad broken record you thought you threw away years ago that has come back to haunt you.

According to *The American Spectator*, pandering is rampant in our government today. Paul Kengor called it like it is—shameless and cynical. He explained, "The Democrats change their ideologies from district to district, from man to man and woman to woman." People running for office are begging for your vote by promising to give you things. What surprises me is that you believe them. I'm not saying that Republicans are much better. The important thing is that you know the quality of the information spoon-fed to you. I'm impressed by some of our Millennials, including Ben Shapiro and Joe Rogan, who can cut through the jargon to get to the core story. Ben is a tireless hero for truth. He walks the independent walk better than anyone I have found online or in the media. I am a true fan, especially when he dares to talk to those who disagree with him at college campuses. Joe really tries to understand the current culture and beliefs. He has an inquisitive mind that all of us should emulate.

CHAPTER 27
What About Congress?

I was fooled when the media first threw mud at Donald Trump. I won't be fooled again. Only a businessman could have made so many improvements in such a short period of time. What we need in the presidency are people who know how to get things done. We need people who understand the poor and how to get them off social services. We need financial and accounting wizards to help the poor, not fleece them for another buck. We need to build each other up and grow our communities again.

The statement "a more perfect union" expects us to continue to strive for the values and morals which served as a guideline for our beautiful country. Our country has increased trade, eliminated slavery, defended the free world, provided for our oldest and most honorable veterans, and supported the infirm and sickly that were in need. Gandhi said, "A nation's greatness can be measured by how it treats its weakest members." This nation and this administration must truly be great based upon that measure. The current administration has cut taxes, decreased trade deficits, provided medical care for its veterans, decreased regulations to allow for increased commerce, increased jobs by increasing commerce, and increased the strengths of the citizen's rights.

The only concern I have with the current administration is the rhetoric. Confrontation might be a habit, but that doesn't make it the best form of communication for a president of the United States. If you ease up, they will come.

Division is evident in the United States Congress, where compromise has become a four-letter word. Fighting between parties can be expected in a bicameral system. Deceit and unsubstantiated accusations are far beyond mere fighting. How, then, should the American people act when their elected leaders choose to squabble over trivialities? Peaceful protest is not enough. Voting out the bad actors only brings new bodies with the same old money. We need term limits. We need accountability. We need the representatives to vote for the will of the populace, not for money. We need to legislate a balanced budget. We need to limit the power and size of the federal government. For all of these reasons, I support a Convention of States—a gathering that would provide a new pathway to fix federal problems—to amend the Constitution. We should not allow this opportunity to fix our system of government to pass us by. Now is the time. It's the only way to prevent future bad actors from attempting another presidential coup. This is the only way to avoid the slavery of our grandchildren to a national debt they cannot pay off.

Our Founding Fathers wrote Article V of the Constitution to allow later generations a chance to rewrite the Constitution. They knew that our republic would fall just like every other republic in history, if we did not have a chance to revolutionize our system periodically. Our Constitution is currently a 10-pound binder with thousands of court cases, which ultimately give unreserved control over us as citizens. The government bureaucracy loves this, because it gives them control over you. If you don't believe me, go ahead and order a copy from our government.

Our republic has become a bloated bureaucracy with limited rule of law. We need to take back our country, and we need to fight for what the Founding Fathers fought for—freedom. This time, God willing, we will have a peaceful transition from bureaucracy back to republic. You know you want term limits for Congress. The data shows we are overwhelmingly in favor of it. What about representation? Did your states' electors vote for the president that won your state? I'll tell you that a record seven electors did not vote for the candidate that won the respective state. I believe that is due to division in our country as much as misrepresentation (see the Federalist Papers). Do you want a balanced budget and spending cuts? If so, you should read Article V of the constitution and check out the call for a

Convention of States. Your decision must be based upon the facts, because it affects this entire country. In fact, since the rest of the world looks to the United States for direction, your decision actually affects the entire world.

If the DNC actually wants to win the presidency and keep control of the House of Representatives, they should pass legislation using compromise to reach across the aisle. They should stop the ridiculous call for impeachment. They should work with the president to pass infrastructure bills and gun registration bills. If John McCain could work with Barack Obama, don't you think Nancy Pelosi could work with Donald Trump?

I pray that my words will have value and will move our moral compass forward. I leave you with a poem I wrote while contemplating Lady Liberty and the national politics of 2019:

Innocence Lost

> My torch is lit
> The flag held high
> Waved in love
> Awake, alive
>
> The power of love
> A clarion call of peace
> Storm clouds approach
> tears of love at my feet
>
> We are at the crossroads
> no left, no right
> only that soft gentle voice
> urging us forward in the night
>
> Rise, fiery phoenix
> Soar, great eagle
> Strike fear into the sinner
> Be our protector

Send forth your Refiner's fire
with the power of love in your hands
Remove the shackles of our fear
Among these shifting sands

None are blameless
All are lost
Look to Him
Your rock, your savior

Author Bio

Stephen Grant has a master's in business finance and engineering management from the University of Michigan. He is a manufacturing engineer, blogger, and author of the new novel America's Culture War: Di-Vision 2020. His second book is a children's book called *The Three Brother Bears* expected out in 2020.

A professionally trained engineer, Stephen has spent the last 25 years managing people, processes, and machinery. His writing comes from firsthand experience of the politics and culture within Fortune 100 corporations. His writing reflects a Christian family perspective towards cultural clashes in our country today.

Stephen and his wife, Dana, have raised foster children in their house for six years, and they adopted two boys in 2016. Stephen volunteers with the Rotary Club of Mississippi and coaches youth soccer.

Made in United States
Cleveland, OH
17 April 2026